The Best Possible World

# THE BEST POSSIBLE WORLD

## A Search for the Nature of Heaven

KELLY J. McCLEARY

ISBN: 978-1-59298-444-2
Library of Congress Control Number: 2011937512

Printed in the United States of America
First Printing: 2012
16   15   14   13   12        5   4   3   2   1

Book design by Mayfly Design

Beaver's Pond Press, Inc.
7104 Ohms Lane, Suite 101, Edina, MN 55439-2129
(952) 829-8818 • www.BeaversPondPress.com
To order, visit www.BeaversPondBooks.com
or call (800) 901-3480. Reseller discounts available.

*To Russ, Bryan, Megan, and Claire,
who taught me the full meaning of love.*

*And to Lon, who now knows
what he did for all of us.*

# Contents

# Prologue

*Then the Lord put forth his hand, and touched my mouth.*
*And the Lord said unto me, Behold, I have put my words*
*in thy mouth.*

—Jeremiah 1:9

A few years ago, as a thirty-seven-year-old mother of two young children, I was suddenly handed a medical diagnosis that was essentially a death sentence. Abruptly forced to examine my life up to that point, I moved several steps along on my faith journey, supported by an outpouring of love from family and friends. Then just as suddenly as it came, the death sentence was lifted, and I moved on with my life, though somewhat differently than I had before.

Fast-forward five years.

A friend recently told me of her discovery of a path in the woods behind her home in the Minnesota countryside where she has lived for four years. While the property through which the path cuts does not belong to her, its discovery was a personal joy, leading her to take peaceful walks in the quiet snow. I feel as though I, too, accidentally discovered my own serene path writing this book. How did I come to write about the nature of heaven? The truth is, I am a skeptic. Not so much a skeptic about the existence of God, as I have somehow always believed in him, but more as a searcher continually trying to find him.

My faith has come as a slow journey over many years; I've made my way as if blind. I don't feel God's presence on a daily basis, and I've never felt especially close to God. I didn't grow up in the church, I haven't studied the Bible, and I don't attend Sunday school. I am an accountant, driven by facts and skeptical of all that can't be factually proven. I am far from an obvious author for a book like this one, and my journey to writing it was appropriately unusual. Although I don't regularly feel God's presence, he has spoken to me exactly three times in my life. This book is the direct result of the last of those three times.

# Chapter 1
# The Search for Heaven

*The human heart refuses to believe in a universe without a purpose.*

—Immanual Kant

Heaven is elusive. Since the beginning of human consciousness, we have speculated about whether we continue to exist after death and, if so, about the nature of that existence. Is the nature of heaven even knowable? There are no facts for us to examine; no witnesses, save a few souls with unverifiable near-death experiences; and a wide range of beliefs about the subject. Are we left only to consider the particular legends of our own culture and accept, reject, or modify them to fit with our own beliefs? Or is it possible that we can know a good deal about the nature of heaven—from this side of it?

Any consideration of heaven must also consider the existence of God. A belief in a wonderful afterlife without a belief in God seems to be fantasy. Believing that God exists prompts us to consider the question of our relation to him and his feelings toward us, including the inevitable question of what he has in mind for our ultimate destiny. To make an exploration of heaven plausible, this book assumes that an omnipotent God—the creator of the universe—exists.

Many religions describe God as just. A just God implies a consistent God, since justice brings a standard against which we will be judged. A consistent God creates the possibility of a consistent existence, that is, one that is consistent with God's essence. It seems reasonable that a consistent God would have created our home similar to his own. Of course it is also possible that Earth and human existence consist of a great God experiment, a divine mad scientist's laboratory entirely divorced from the true nature of God. That would, however, preclude a splendid opportunity for God to provide us an opportunity to better understand him. Though God could certainly have made us unable to understand him, we clearly do possess the ability to ponder the reason behind our existence. This ability makes it plausible that he has chosen to be at least somewhat transparent. A consistent and transparent God is the second assumption on which we will base our search for the nature of heaven.

## What Do Religions Say about Heaven?

Dealing with the nature of heaven requires dealing with the nature of both human existence and hell. A primary purpose of organized religion is to explain the nature of this life and what happens after death, whether in heaven, hell or some other place. The world's religions deal with heaven in vastly different ways: Some are very descriptive about what heaven (and hell) will be like, while others are intentionally vague.

Let's start near the beginning.

Thousands of years ago, Zoroastrianism, an ancient Persian religion with few current adherents and centered primarily in Iran, emerged at the then-center of civilization. The influence of this little-known religion is still evident today in many of the world's major religions, including in their understanding of the nature of God, hell, and heaven. Predating Judaism, Islam, and Christianity, Zoroastrianism promoted belief in a divine dualism: a god of good (Ahura Mazda) and a god of evil (Angra Mainyu). Zoroastrianism is also the source of the term "paradise," whose root "pa-ri-daeza" means a walled park or garden in the ancient Persian language.[1] Finally, it held a materialistic view of the afterlife, including very detailed descriptions of both the pleasures of the garden and the torments of the fire, a belief that Islam adopted.[2]

In contrast, Judaism and Christianity are more ambiguous about the nature of heaven. The Jewish picture of heaven is aligned with the faith's general outlook; heaven is a quiet and peaceful place filled with intellectual activity.[3] Christian denominations hold varying views about heaven. While medieval Catholicism viewed heaven as a physical place, currently that view is less clearly endorsed, with many Catholics today believing instead that heaven is a condition of the soul.[4] Similarly, Eastern Orthodoxy maintains that heaven and hell are states of the soul: Heaven is paradise, and hell the torment of judgment.[5]

At least two major world religions, Buddhism and Hinduism, have very different conceptions of heaven and hell. Buddhists believe in an infinite cycle of death and rebirth, all filled with suffering. The quality of each rebirth is directly related to actions in a person's previous life. Even the best rebirth leads to another cycle of suffering and death; the only escape is enlightenment, at which point the cycle ends and heaven is achieved.[6] Though Hindus believe in a "heaven" (*svarga*), which can be the reward for the practice of good deeds, it is only a temporary resting place; once a person's merit is used up, back to Earth he will go, in a constant cycle of rebirth driven by the karma he has created in his lives.[7]

While views about heaven vary, most world faiths believe that death is followed by *something* ... generally something good for a life well lived and often something bad for a life lived poorly.

The Christian Bible includes a multitude of references to heaven, though they are short on details. The Bible tells us that heaven is a truly glorious place, that "eye hath not seen, nor ear heard, neither have entered into the heart of man, the things which God hath prepared for them that love him."[8] The most tangible description is perhaps the well-known verse, "In My Father's house are many mansions; if it were not so, I would have told you."[9] While this familiar passage refers to human dwellings, other passages seem to indicate a divine, not earthly, condition: "For the kingdom of God is not meat and drink; but righteousness, and peace, and joy in the Holy Ghost."[10] Other passages describe heaven as belonging to God;[11] existing for the glory of God;[12] and promised to us as our ultimate reward.[13]

Jesus is quoted in a number of passages talking about the kingdom of heaven, though usually in parable form. Jesus, for example, tells us that heaven will be magnificent, comparing it to a great treasure[14] and a pearl of great price.[15] The Bible also speaks to who can expect to end up in heaven and in hell: "People are judged according to the light, according to the awareness of opportunities they have had" and there are "degrees of rewards and punishment."[16] In the Book of Revelations, Jesus promises "to him who overcomes I will give to eat from the tree of life, which is in the midst of the Paradise of God."[17] Further, Jesus states that the sinful "will go away into everlasting punishment, but the righteous into eternal life"[18] and informs us there will be a ranking in heaven, that those keeping the commandments will be called greatest in the kingdom of heaven[19].

Jesus also lists at least one requirement—humility—for getting into heaven.[20] And he makes it clear that not everyone will enter into heaven and that those who do not will suffer.[21] In the parable of the separation of the wheat and the chaff, Jesus says that God will "burn the chaff with unquenchable fire"[22] and at the final judgment, "the angels will come forth, separate the wicked from among the just, and cast them into the furnace of fire. There will be wailing and gnashing of teeth."[23] He also says we should "fear him who is able to destroy both soul and body in hell."[24]

So the abundant biblical references leave much to be desired in the way of details about heaven, and even those that the Bible provides are open to interpretation. The obvious reality is this: No one knows for sure. We have no witnesses, no indisputable facts. A religion's prophets or holy texts may claim to offer the truth about the afterlife, but who can factually argue or agree? While most faiths believe there is *something* after death, just what that something *is* is simultaneously critical to know and yet unknowable.

Most faiths also believe that *the something* that exists for us after death is good (so long as we have been good), and that it is good in a way that is comparable to earthly goodness. While comparing the good of heaven to the good on Earth may be simply constructing an ideal from what we know, we must consider the reverse possibility—that heaven reminds us of the good on Earth because *the good on Earth is a reflection of heaven.*

This view is broadly held. Christian Scientists believe that the elements of heaven are always present and that we occasionally get glimpses of the true reality in moments of particular beauty and awe.[25] The Quaker author Elton Trueblood said that "all the world is one house, and that if we move out of the present room of our finite existence, we are not thereby going out from under the loving care of the Father's roof but only into another and perhaps a more wonderful room."[26] Even Plato described this life as "the best possible world. It is the fairest of things that come to be, its maker is good, it is fashioned after the most perfect model, and it is as like that model as possible."[27] What we search for is an understanding of that most perfect model upon which our "best possible world" was based.

### Is the Answer Right in Front of Us?

Human beings seek meaning to our existence. In that search for meaning, cultures have integrated spirituality and gods into belief systems since the time we have possessed the consciousness that makes us human. Examples are plentiful and often tangible, from prehistoric cave paintings, to the Nasca geoglyphs in Peru, to the Sistine Chapel. Our individual actions, ranging from everyday acts of charity to extraordinary acts of martyrdom for causes we deeply believe in, demonstrate our faith in something beyond ourselves. Many philosophers and theologians maintain that this universal longing for meaning is compelling evidence of a God that wants to be found. This is the third and final assumption in our search.

If God wants to be found, then why doesn't he just directly reveal himself to us? God could choose to provide constant and unmistakable evidence of his presence to ensure that we find him. Genesis says that God chose to make us in his image, and the most important element of that image may be the singular aspect that separates us from animals: free will with a sense of morality. Alone among God's creatures, we have the capacity to choose what will guide our lives and to understand right from wrong. It is plausible to believe that if God made it easy for us to see him on a daily basis, then we would lose our ability to choose him. By staying just hidden, God allows us to have free will.[28] By making us incomplete without him, we have a deep need to find meaning, to search for him.

Given the diversity of cultures and human personalities, it is reasonable to assume that God needs a variety of methods to draw us to him. This variety can be seen even within Christian denominations, let alone across the world's major religions. Individuals seek meaning from a variety of sources, although these sources seem to fall into three broad categories. First, there are people who are driven by logic. The world's scientists, mathematicians, and engineers seek order in every aspect of their lives and find meaning and comfort in that order. Second, there are the artists. They search for meaning from beauty in multiple forms: music, sculpture, architecture, fashion, and design. Finally there are the relaters. These emotional "feelers" place the strongest emphasis on their relationships with others. While for most of us one of these three primary aspects dominates, we all draw meaning from and have incomplete lives without some measure of all three: order, beauty, and love.

Why order, beauty, and love? If our search for meaning routinely includes the pursuit of these three aspects of our world and existence, then it is possible that God uses our yearning for these as an indirect means to help us find him. Since he desires to have us find him, he needs ways for us to seek, discover, ponder, and comprehend him. Given the diversity in our cultures and personalities, the wider the variety of methods to reach us, the better the odds we will succeed in understanding their message.

It is plausible, then, that after designing us to require meaning, God fills our lives with example after example of order, beauty, and love so that we consistently stumble upon these examples and comprehend their link back to him. Taking this hypothesis one final step, order, beauty, and love may not just be critical pieces of a puzzle leading to a very important solution, but also ways for us to find meaning in *aspects of God's very nature.* Having us find him through his very nature would be a meaningful way for us to develop and deepen our relationship with him. As we begin to understand the nature of God, we can begin to speculate on the nature of his home.

To recap our three foundational assumptions: God exists, God is consistent, and God wants to be found. He made us with a need to find meaning, and he has left us with ways to find him if we will but look. The three organizational sections of this book—order, beauty, and love—present evidence of some of the clues that God appears to have scattered throughout our world for us to find and that will give us a better understanding of him. Each part will provide reasons why we need not depend solely on religious beliefs, but can study our own experience to learn about the nature of heaven. Current thinking in a number of fields is beginning to support evidence for a divine "echo" in our world; we will examine some of these echoes. Once we know they are there, we can see them everywhere.

# Part One
# Order

# Chapter 2
# The Beauty of Science
(Otherwise Known as "The Put-Up Job")

*Why are things as they are and not otherwise?*
—Johannes Kepler

Simply put, science is the study of the way things are. The ancient Greeks are generally identified as the first scientists, as they were the first to distinguish between the natural and the supernatural, recognizing that natural phenomena are the predictable outcome of cause and effect, as opposed to the will of the gods.[29] Aristotelian science strove to explain *why* things happen, while modern science was born when Galileo began to try to explain *how* things happen.[30]

The birth of modern science was revolutionary in that it appeared to break the link between God and natural phenomena. This perceived attack caused the

Catholic Church to pronounce Galileo a heretic for proclaiming that the Earth was not the center of the universe. It is ironic that today many prominent scientists increasingly believe they see evidence of God's hand in the astonishingly complex workings of our world. Many of them, in a multitude of fields, are beginning to publicly discuss this possibility. Collectively, a variety of disciplines provide tantalizing evidence of some kind of intelligent design at work in our universe. We will explore the evidence behind two of these areas of interest.

Technology is one of the hallmarks of our species, evolving millennia ago with the development of our first crude tools and progressing spectacularly with the ancient Chinese, Egyptians, and Babylonians, who built great civilizations on the back of amazing technological advances. More recently, the Industrial and Information Revolutions have driven further explosions of technology, and their ingenious fruits naturally cause us to consider what motivates us to push for these advances, and why we are curious enough to try to explain the world around us.

To tackle this question, let's distinguish between science and technology. While technology is the practical application of scientific discovery, often for practical or economic purposes, science is discovery for discovery's sake. Given its practical purpose, technology is a logical outcome of human effort: it is understandable that humans pursue activities that make their lives better. Pure science is not as easily explained. Certainly some science is driven by expected benefits, but why do we seek knowledge for knowledge sake?

While scientific inquiry is the best way to understand the world around us, it likely won't answer any of the big questions, like "Why are we here?" or "What happens after we die?"[31] Great philosophers have pondered why we engage in pure science for centuries. Plato and Aristotle, for example, believed that the study of nature is the only true path to happiness, revealing the beauty and order of the universe and helping a person develop his character.[32]

In their book *A Meaningful World*, Benjamin Wiker and Jonathan Witt recognize "the drive to understand, not for any ulterior motive, but purely for the sake of knowing."[33] At the root of the human urge to understand our world lies a critical and inherent assumption: A fundamental order must exist that makes it possible to find predictive root causes. A random world would have rendered pure science impossible.

According to Wiker and Witt, "Essential to scientific progress was a kind of continual correlation between the unshakable conviction that there is some underlying order in nature waiting to be discovered and the actual presence of an underlying order in nature."[34] Without that order, our quest for understanding would be quickly frustrated and science would have been long abandoned.

Not long ago, it was widely believed that technological advances would cause a decline in religion, and the nineteenth century saw paradigm-changing ideas with the power to do just that.[35] The publication of Darwin's *Origin of Species* proposed a vastly older Earth than previously believed. This new theory posed a significant challenge to deeply held Christian beliefs. Unlike Galileo's sun-centered solar system centuries before, the idea took hold that science—not God—might explain life's big questions.

Social changes early in the twentieth century, including the influential ideas of Freud and Marx and the massive bloodshed of two world wars, only seemed to echo Nietzsche's declaration that "God is dead." Yet an unexpected scientific development in the middle of the twentieth century began to raise suspicion that God's obituary was premature. This important discovery occurred in the biggest science, astronomy, which attempts to answer *what is out there.*

Plato had been the first to insist that astronomy should be treated as a science and could be modeled using geometry.[37] Plato's belief in a mathematical structure of the universe was one of his most important ideas. Today's advanced study of astronomy, aided by the use of powerful telescopes and sophisticated physics, may seem of little use to most people. However, astronomy has long been useful to agriculture, navigation, and the military, ensuring its early importance as a field of study.[38] And one of its most commonly studied objects, Earth's moon, has given us inquisitive inhabitants of Earth important pieces to the puzzle that is our universe.

In fact, studying the moon is extraordinarily ideal in aiding in the advancement of our understanding of the universe. Solar eclipses provided ancient verification of the predicted movement of celestial bodies, as well as proof of Einstein's theory of relativity. Only an incredible coincidence, namely that the sun is four hundred times larger than the moon while also four hundred times farther away, enables these vital phenomenon to occur at all.[39] We are indeed lucky to have just the tool needed to enable some of the most

important advancements in furthering our understanding of the universe.

A big breakthrough came with what is now
known as the Big Bang theory. First put forward
around 1930 as a result of evidence of an expanding
universe, eighty years of subsequent study have yield-
ed an understanding of how finely tuned the laws and
constants of the cosmos are; astrophysicists now realize that even small changes in these fundamentals
would render life as we know it impossible.[40] For example, gravity and the forces causing the expansion
of the universe are nearly perfectly balanced.[41] If the
balance between the outward energy of expansion and
the gravitational forces trying to pull everything back
together again were off by more than one part in $10^{59}$,
the universe would be unrecognizable and would never have sustained life.[42]

Too much energy, and the matter in the universe
would have widely dispersed, unable to come together. Too little energy, and the universe would have col-
lapsed back onto itself.[43] Altogether there are fifteen
physical constants—including the speed of light; the
force of gravity; the weak and strong nuclear forces;
and various aspects of electromagnetism—whose values are "given," hence the term "constant." These fixed

values lay the foundation for the precise nature of our universe. The odds that all fifteen of them would have naturally landed at exactly their given values, which happen to be required to create our universe, are unbelievably and remotely small.[44]

Are we just a lucky fluke of nature? In 1973, a Cambridge astrophysicist, Brandon Carter, wrote a paper in which he pointed out that all of the crucial rules in physics seem to have one thing in common: they appear precisely designed to create a universe capable of producing life.[45] The idea was astonishing to mainstream modern science and became increasingly discussed among conventional scientists. Though publicly not believing in a divinely created universe or in heaven, the famous astrophysicist Stephen Hawking said, "It would be very difficult to explain why the universe should have begun in just this way, except as the act of a God who intended to create beings like us."[46] The cosmologist (and atheist) Fred Hoyle, facing the growing scientific evidence of intricate design, called the universe a "put-up job."[47] According to Freeman Dyson, the theoretical physicist and mathematician, "This is a universe that knew we were coming."[48]

The great challenge posed by the Big Bang theory is the theological dilemma it creates: What was there *before* the moment of creation?[49] The Big Bang theory itself declares that the universe had a clear beginning, which, as the famed geneticist Francis Collins points out, "cries out for a divine explanation."[50] In spite of growing scientific evidence, Einstein refused to accept the Big Bang theory for a decade because it posed this very question.[51] While future discoveries in astrophysics are inevitable, on this momentous issue we have already reached the ultimate limit of science and reason; neither can reach back before the moment of creation to determine the universe's first cause.

# Chapter 3
# The Image of God

*The bad part of it, especially for me, lies in the fact that
science of all things seems to demand the existence of God.*
—Sigmund Freud

The German philosopher Immanuel Kant believed
that a random scientific order could explain everything except two things: life and beauty.[52] We will
leave beauty to Part Two of this book and deal now
with life. In the last chapter, we saw that the universe
seems to have been perfectly designed for sustaining
life. Is there similar evidence supporting a divine design of life itself?

Just as a number of amazing coincidences set a
life-enabling universe in motion, Earth, too, seems
ideally suited for life in a number of ways. Astrobi-
ologists now generally assume that life must be based

on carbon, a substance found abundantly in our planet's crust. Scientists also believe that water is necessary for life.[53] Oxygen, required for water, is relatively common on Earth. Our orbit around the sun is only slightly elliptical, critical to Earth's staying within the life-sustaining warmth of the sun.

So our home is ready for life; what next? Let's start with a promising scientific breakthrough that occurred fifty years ago. In famous experiments, Stanley Miller and Harold Urey were able to build small quantities of amino acids, the basic building blocks of life, by applying an electrical charge to water and organic compounds. Though initially these experiments generated hope that we could find the mechanism to artificially create life, repeated attempts over the last fifty years have dead-ended in spite of tremendous advances in biology over that same period.[54]

If we can't spontaneously create life in a test tube, what first sparked it in the laboratory that was early Earth? Obviously, we may yet discover this secret and finally complete the Miller-Urey experiments. It is also possible that we have not created life because we never can, that it is a feat belonging solely to God.

Astonishing progress has been made in revealing the mystery of life. The discovery of DNA in 1953 by Watson and Crick created a whole new discipline of science that finally solved the mechanism for Darwin's evolution. Here, too, God seems to be quietly slipping in as scientists unlock DNA's mysteries. Harvard paleontologist Stephen Jay Gould has questioned how evolution alone could explain the diversity of life seen mushrooming in the fossil record 550 million years ago. Known as the "Cambrian explosion," this period saw a large number of new invertebrates preceded by only single-celled organisms in the fossil record.[55] Gould believes that the fossil record does not support the steady changes hypothesized by Darwin, but instead shows long periods of stability followed by bursts of significant change—something not totally accounted for by natural selection.[56]

Other scientists do not agree, believing the fossil record does support "smooth" transitions. For believers who hold that God and evolution can coexist, there are multiple views about how God may have directed the tremendous proliferation of life on Earth. Some believe that God was the initial cause of life and then let natural forces he set into motion take over. Others believe that he intervened in evolutionary forces to ensure his desired results transpired. Yet others believe he kicked off an evolutionary process guided by his own master design.[57] Of course, an omnipotent God would certainly be capable of creating life any way he wished. While it remains unsettled, the debate raises the possibility of some sort of divine intervention in the evolution of life toward human beings.

Let's look more closely at the science behind DNA to determine if faith in God is incompatible with belief in evolution. Human beings, along with most other life forms, are born with significantly more DNA than seems required. We may yet find some purpose behind this unused DNA, but currently the vast majority of DNA sequences appear to be non-functioning.[58] It is believed these nonfunctioning sequences were caused by mutations. Most genetic mutations are unfavorable for the conditions of life and are therefore not passed on.[59] But many mutations are not so unfavorable that they cause *us* to die out, and so we pass them on to our offspring. Some of these mutations, known as *ancient repetitive elements* (AREs), were truncated when replicated, leaving them nonfunctional. Human and mice DNA share virtually identical segments of AREs—in the same locations. The comparison between human and chimpanzee genes is even closer; 96 percent is identical at the DNA level and once again include identical

AREs. Sharing a common ancestor is a logical explanation for this commonality.[60]

One could ask why mutations exist at all, since it is at least equally plausible that genetic copies would be perfect.[61] Yet without these built-in mistakes, we would not have evolved. Then there are the billions of other seemingly chance events that led to us. For example, without the Chicxulub asteroid impact in the Yucatan Peninsula sixty-five million years ago—an event that is widely believed to have caused the death of the dinosaurs—mammals would not have flourished and, once again, we would not be here.[62]

But we *are* here.

Genesis says that God created us in his own image, implying that, in some way, we resemble God. Scientists point to language, the ability to know right from wrong, self-awareness, and the ability to imagine the future as the primary characteristics distinguishing humans from animals.[63] Perhaps in one of these characteristics we resemble God. The Harvard professor Owen Gingerich proposes that the primary elements of God's image reflected in us are creativity, conscience, and consciousness.[64] Whichever elements we focus on, we are alone on our planet in our ability to explore our surroundings, discover the forces that make it work, and ponder the meaning of it all.

Nature and its close cousin, science, can neither prove nor disprove God's existence; they can only help point to what it all may mean.[65] While we cannot reason our way to a belief in God, science has developed enough over the last fifty years to no longer present an obstacle to that belief.[66] Some prominent contemporary scientists are even beginning to argue for the contrary: that science may be beginning to point toward a divine design and purpose evident in our universe. In this way, they circle back to earlier scientific thinkers. Scientists such as Copernicus, Galileo, Kepler, and Newton believed their work supported a belief in God, that the more we understood about the workings of the universe, the more we could understand its maker.[67]

Einstein studied the order in the universe, calling this search "his longing to understand what God was thinking,"[68] though to Einstein "God" was a shortcut concept. Francis Collins, the doctor and geneticist who led the International Human Genome Project that mapped the entire human DNA, called DNA, together with mathematics, "the language of God."[69] The fact that we have massive evidence for the Big Bang and evolution does not mean that we must discard religious beliefs. We can turn to our ability to reason and interpret what Timothy Keller calls the "clues of God" around us.[70] If we believe in God, the clues make sense. If we don't, our reasoning leads us to believe that he does not exist, and then we do not expect God's clues—they make no sense.[71]

Galileo, in a letter to Grand Duchess Christina in 1605, said, "I do not feel obliged to believe that the same God who has endowed me with sense, reason, and intellect has intended us to forgo their use." He felt that the world provided evidence for God's existence and that human reason, when considering this evidence, would conclude that God, as people understood him, existed. If we who concur with Galileo are wrong, and the universe doesn't provide evidence for God as we understand him, we are left with at least two options. Maybe the intricate order in our universe is an astounding, miraculous accident. Or perhaps the evidence we see pointing to a grand design for our universe is only a colossal joke played on us by God—planting fossils, radioactive decay, and genomes around us to test our faith.[72]

But just maybe the clues scattered throughout the universe and revealed by our scientific discoveries actually point to God behind the design. As Professor

Gingerich said, while scientific evidence doesn't prove the existence of God, "the universe makes more sense with this understanding."[73] We believe we see order in our world around us and are driven to find it. When we find order, we gain insight, into ourselves and the workings of our world. As our understanding of our world increases, we are eventually able—if our faith allows it—to see the hand of God in its making.

# A Reflection on Order

*The universal order and the personal order are nothing but different expressions and manifestations of a common underlying principle.*

—Marcus Aurelius

My father is bipolar, although he wasn't diagnosed until I was seventeen. My mother says that, in hindsight, the diagnosis made many things make sense. I have no idea how many jobs my dad had when I was growing up, but he once told me that he liked starting over with a clean slate. By the time I was ten, we were living in my sixth house. We were fortunate to have my mother, the rock in our family. The reserved daughter of a German Mennonite, she provided us with a stable emotional and financial foundation, something my family needed given my dad's illness.

When he wasn't sick, Dad was a lot of fun. My sister and I organized our slumber parties around his schedule so that he could provide the entertainment for our friends. But there were times when things spiraled out of control. This may be why I am drawn to order, to finding comfort in the predictability of science and numbers. I've always searched for the answer to why things are as they are. I want to understand the relationships between everything and everything else: How have ancient historical events impacted current ones? How do sociological theories drive macroeconomic behavior? How does higher-order math move toward philosophy but remain orderly and predictable?

I started on this search for explanation when I was very young. For example, when I was six, I wanted to be an astronaut. When I was ten, I read my mother's childhood set of 1956 encyclopedias. It was during the Carter administration, and the books stopped at Ike, but I didn't care: They contained huge quantities of fascinating information on history and geography and science. I couldn't get enough.

By high school, I was reading scientific periodicals and wanted to be a theoretical physicist or a medical researcher. Then I met my husband and the rest, as they say, is history. We married young, and I majored in something practical, although still orderly: finance. I still read nonfiction avidly and am driven to learn, to understand the infinite relationships all around us. And it seems that nearly everything *can* be connected to nearly everything else. Recognizing this, I am in awe. My revelation in writing this book is that while I had expected the hard sciences to be orderly, I never imagined that so-called softer subjects like art, music, and even the biology of love could provide evidence for, of all things, God.

It is a myth—or at least a mistaken assumption—that religion and science are necessarily incompatible.[74] A century after religion was declared dead at the hands of science, many scientific disciplines increasingly point to evidence of an intelligent design. The incomprehensible fine-tuning of the universe, the awesome complexity and beauty of DNA, the final mysteries of life's "spark," and whatever existed before the Big Bang remain amazing mysteries. Science can answer many of our questions, but some are destined to go unanswered.

Why are we driven to ask the big questions of life? Why does the universe not only seem ideally designed for our existence, but also provide us with unending opportunities to explore, to search for some meaning in it all? We are conscious. We are the only creatures on Earth who know that we exist and who know that we will die. That knowledge leaves us with a fundamental choice: to believe that all of this, including our own existence, is a colossal accident that will cease to exist when we cease to exist; or, guided by our hearts, to consider the evidence around us as telling us there is an intelligent design behind this grand, intricate, and astonishing creation.

Timothy Keller posed a great question: While technically all the apparent fine-tuning for life in the universe could have happened without a creator, does it make sense to live our lives based on that remote chance?[75] Centuries before the formulation of the Big Bang theory, St. Thomas foreshadowed it, describing a first cause for which no cause can be given and "to which everyone gives the name of God."[76]

# Part Two

# Beauty

# Chapter 4
# Why Art?

*He was enjoying one of those moments of selfish,*
*exclusive, supreme pleasure, during which the artist sees*
*nothing in the world but art, and sees the world in art.*
—Victor Hugo

In our search for meaning, we have long embedded art into our spiritual life. The great art historian H. W. Janson called art "the universal language,"[77] defining four criteria that make art just that: art. They are the following:

1.  Art is *created* by an artist's hand, not a naturally occurring phenomenon.
2.  Art is a creation of the artist's *imagination*.
3.  Art is an *original creation*, distinguished from crafts, which are mass copied.

4. Art relies on *tradition*. All artists borrow thoughts and ideas from others, but in so doing, create something new.[78]

Art is meant to be representational and inspirational, symbolizing our most important ideas sometimes so tangibly that we worship the created object itself. In European culture prior to the Renaissance, art was a primary means of communicating to the illiterate masses the messages of their faith. The stained glass windows and statues in Gothic churches, for example, told nearly all of the stories most of the congregants knew.[79]

The grandest example of art's spiritual symbolism is architecture. As substantial alterations of the physical environment, buildings and monuments display a society's beliefs and values in a relatively permanent way. Noteworthy examples are numerous, and include the Egyptian pyramids, Cambodia's Angkor Wat, and Paris's Cathedral of Notre Dame. Architecture on this scale consumes an enormous amount of a society's energy and resources, toward an end that often does not directly benefit the masses of that society.

What would persuade a civilization to dedicate significant resources for the decades or even centuries needed to construct such monuments? Economic incentives in the form of jobs for workers and craftsmen are clearly part of the appeal. However, job creation isn't enough to explain the inspiration for history's great temples and cathedrals. Victor Hugo expressed his belief in the ultimate importance of architecture in *The Hunchback of Notre Dame*:

> Architecture was, up to the fifteenth century, the chief register of humanity; that during this space of time no idea of any elaboration appeared in the world without being built into masonry; that every popular idea as well as every religious law has had its monument in fact, that the human race has never had an important thought which it has not written in stone.[80]

Because monuments express our most important ideas, they are worthy of the careful design and artistic expression that we put into them.

Why do we value art for its own sake, and why do individuals regularly create it, often without any commercial incentive? Art may have helped early humans thrive or even to have survived. The great anthropologist Claude Levi-Strauss believed that art plays an important role in culture by helping groups define themselves and allowing individuals to define themselves in relation to the group.[81] Art contributes to the collective experience of a community, and a cohesive community helps individuals survive under adversity.[82]

Since art endures beyond its creators, it also continues or passes down a culture's values.[83] One of the simplest and earliest ways of passing on a culture has been through artists creating everyday objects with meanings particular to that culture.[84] Historically, even ordinary household objects such as food vessels, ornaments, and clothing that were adorned with art were used ritualistically and socially, and reflected the needs and values of that society.[85] Given their artistic and cultural significance, everyday objects were crafted with such care that today we value them and place them in our museums.[86]

Museums as public institutions are a fairly recent invention, evolving to display a community's artistic greatness as well as the spoils of its military conquests. A society's museums, galleries and opera houses show its cultural superiority and its willingness to spend its resources on the support of art. Many people laud museums for throwing wide open the world of art to average modern humans.[87] Some argue, however, that museums remove art from daily life, thus removing it from its cultural context.[88] They believe that we cannot fully understand art from other cultures and times, since we cannot fully understand the role it played with its maker and users.

Capitalism has also changed our connection to art by initiating the creation of art for the sole purpose of being sold, collected by those looking for visible ways to show off their wealth.[89] In response, some artists in developed economics, removed from the ordinary flow of social services, feel the need to show that financial interests do not drive them to create. To demonstrate their independence, they set themselves apart through eccentric behavior, further isolating art from mainstream society.[90] According to Levi-Strauss, contemporary art only adds to this separation by breaking from reality. Many people in our culture cannot relate to modern art, divorced as it is from everyday human experience.[91]

Further distancing most people from beauty—especially the kind of beauty that inspires art—modern life, with its factories, nondescript apartment buildings, and pollution is disfiguring our environment. Our surroundings are now increasingly ugly, weakening our daily link to art.[92] In spite of these challenges, modern times have also created new areas of opportunity in maintaining a personal connection to art. People in today's more affluent societies have significant leisure time in which to create or enjoy the arts, of which many take great advantage. Media such as mass photography and video make new formats for creating art accessible to more of us.

So art has a role in creating and sustaining culture, but what drives *individuals* to create art? One theory is that, given the many inherent dangers in our environment, we are biologically programmed to prefer order and harmony in relation to our surroundings.[93] Art helps us partially create our environment, increasing our comfort level with it.[94] According to some thinkers, the foundation of art, after all, is nature: Greek philosophers believed that art was what tied us to nature,[95] and nineteenth century American landscape artists believed that God speaks to us directly through nature.[96]

Art, too, can help create order by representing experiences symbolically. The German philosopher Ernst Cassirer said we try to capture, explain, and make meaningful our experiences through symbols, often expressed as art.[97] We search for significance and will create it ourselves through art, creating new, artistic objects from the movement, combination, or even destruction of objects within our environment. The new object is created first in our minds, and the artist gains satisfaction from fulfilling that original vision.[98] According to a view such as this, every work of art is, by its nature, an abstraction, a symbol of the artist's subject. The artist decides how much and what parts of the original will be expressed.[99] Artists bring their own experiences, biases, and worldview to their particular talent and interpretation of their surroundings.[100]

We come to this urge to relate symbolically early on. One of a child's most important tasks following infancy is coming to terms with a world of symbols. Language is the earliest and most common example of symbolism, with music close behind.[101] While differences exist between individuals and cultures, the way children progress through the stages of artistic development are remarkably universal.[102] From birth to about two years of age—the sensorimotor stage—children gain a practical knowledge of their world. At two years to about six or seven, children first begin to explore the use of symbols in their world. The concrete-operational stage, from about seven to twelve years of age, is when children can classify and think logically about objects and understand their permanence. By early adolescence, we are able to think about the world in an abstract or theoretical way using words and symbols.[103]

Artistic creativity is especially present in young preschool children as they master the use of symbols both in drawing and in language. As they enter elementary school, this creativity transforms into conformity in most children. They become significantly inhibited and risk averse from an artistic perspective and lose a great deal of their creativity.[104] Before this social inhibition sets in, very young children are the closest to true artists who push us to look at the world as we did when we were children, with wonder and fascination.[105] As Michael Kimmelman says in his book *The Accidental Masterpiece*:

> Maybe this is why artists who push us to look more carefully at simple things may also strike a slightly melancholic note. They remind us of a childlike condition of wonderment that we abandoned once we became adults and that we need art to highlight occasionally, if only to recall for us what we have given up.[106]

It is an interesting thought that there could be a link between art and the biblical verse "unless you change and become like children, you will never enter the Kingdom of heaven."[107]

Art is a paradox: while its creation is a very personal experience, it is often meant to be shared. As Janson notes, "The creative process is not completed until the work has found an audience."[108] For an object to be truly artistic, it must also be aesthetic; that is, it must be meant to be experienced by others.[109] Art is aesthetic when it spurs an emotional reaction in us, which is different for every person who experiences the art every time he experiences it.[110] An artist's goal for his art is typically an attempt to spark a specific emotion or set of emotions in us.[111] In fact, some thinkers believe that a work of art's meaning lies in its ability to stir emotions in us—emotions that arise often because of past experiences—although art's goal is to create a present experience for its viewers.[112]

There appear to be clear reasons for art's existence: it helps define a culture; it symbolizes what is important to us; and it facilitates emotional experiences. However, art seems to bring more meaning to our lives than these explanations fully account for. A work of beauty can bring us wonder, joy, or awe on a scale sometimes large and grand, sometimes small and exquisite. An unexpected architectural surprise, a grand work hanging in a museum, or even a well-formed household object can bring us momentary delight. Why is this? Why should we be driven to create objects we want others to admire, objects that will often outlive us? Why are we, alone among all creatures, drawn to beauty, unnecessary as it is for survival? For some reason, art brings meaning to our lives, making it worth spending the effort beyond the basic necessities of life to create it and experience it. Our early ancestors found it to be so, and thus far we have not evolved beyond it.

# Chapter 5
# Music—Medicine for the Soul

*Music produces a kind of pleasure which human nature cannot do without.*

—Confucius

Music is universal and arguably fundamental to our existence. Musical instruments have been found at some of the world's oldest archaeological sites, and long have been an important part of human tradition and celebration.[113] Greeks even associated music with medicine, believing it to heal the soul just as medicine heals the body.[114] But why is it so important? The development of hearing, the ability to detect and analyze the source of vibrating objects, makes strong evolutionary sense; this ability would have presented a survival advantage.[115] Musical ability would have been a further evolutionary advantage, signaling creativity—a scientifically proven mating preference—in addition to adequate resource wealth.

Another theory supporting musical aptitude as providing an evolutionary advantage is its social purpose.[116] The act of setting words to music played a significant role in passing down stories and histories in prewriting cultures. Entire books can be committed to memory with rhythm, rhyme, and sometimes, tune.[117] In all cultures, music has a role in bringing people together, primarily through rhythm. Rhythm turns listeners into active participants by synchronizing their minds and bodies.[118]

A third argument for music's potential evolutionary advantage is that it is cognitive. Some scientists argue that music may have been the driver to speech development in humans.[119] Children's regular exposure to music, especially through participation, may stimulate brain development, in particular by requiring different areas of the brain to work together to listen to or perform music.[120] Demonstrating the brain's affinity for music, recent studies have shown that even imagining music activates the auditory cortex almost as much as listening to it does.[121]

There is a strong science behind the evolutionary advantages of music. Scientists have learned that our auditory and nervous systems seem perfectly tuned for music.[122] Music's impact on the brain is exact and precise, indicating its importance.[123] Pitch is directly translated to our brain: The vibration frequency of the sound causes electrical activity in our brains to fire at the exact same frequency.[124] Music is so elemental that some of the inputs from the ear are sent not to the auditory complex in the brain, but instead directly to the cerebellum, or primitive "reptilian brain" which controls movement and, scientists believe, possibly emotion.[125] Indeed, music is so primal that for many advanced dementia patients, responding to music is often one of the last mental capacities they have left.[126]

Music impacts a number of regions in the brain, including those involved in the production of pleasure-inducing opioids and dopamine, which helps explain why we derive pleasure from listening to music.[127] Having two ears to process music also seems important. Those who lose hearing in one ear don't hear in stereo; for them, music can lose its emotional appeal.[128] Listening to recorded music with only one earpiece can replicate some sense of their loss.

One does not have to be musical to enjoy music. Responding to music is a fundamental part of being human, and there is no human culture that does not use and value music.[129] We gain comfort from repetition, and with music we obtain the stimulus and reward of repetition. We also experience pleasure when we receive resolution of some emotion.[130] Music creates that resolution by creating suspense through uncertainty of what comes next. We derive pleasure when "what comes next" resolves that uncertainty with our predetermined range of what *should* be next.[131]

Our expectations of what should be next are built on our past experiences; we require a past experience in that style of music to have expectations about it.[132] Composers play on our expectations, deviating from them or choosing an unexpected (though acceptable) alternative. The primary difference between music and visual art is that music develops expectations in the brain over time.[133] Our brain derives pleasure from these expectations, by whether the composer/performer plays on or against them. Normally, unmet expectations cause fear in us; however, we are conditioned that music is not a threat, but a source of pleasure.[134]

Music that is too simple bores us; if it is too complex, we don't have the patience to follow it. We need a happy medium between complex enough to interest us and predictable enough to be familiar.[135] Children start out preferring simple tunes with predictable chord progressions. As we mature, we begin to tire of simpler melodies and seek out more complex melodies.[136] (This is why our children's repeated singing of the same simple tune gets on our nerves.)

Our musical tastes are also shaped by our cultures. Different cultures use different scales, and over time, our brains learn those cultural norms. Without any formal musical training, we gradually learn to detect clues that help us know what the composer intends.[137] We know when a wrong note or an out-of-key note is played, and we know that music in major scales is "happy," while minor scales are "sad." Playing a scale particular to a culture can easily and quickly evoke thoughts of that culture.[138] We also quickly internalize rhythms present in our surroundings. By the age of twelve months, our responses to rhythms have narrowed to those to which we have been repeatedly exposed. By the age of twenty or so, we stop forming new neural connections so rapidly. By adulthood, we have developed preferences for the music of our cultures.[139]

Because they invoke our emotions, art and music are about vulnerability—ours and the artist's. This is one reason the experience of art and music is so personal and we often enjoy it most when alone.[140]

A work of art is recreated every time it is aesthetically experienced. Music is the best example: It is new every time it is experienced, depending on the background, mood, and prior experiences of the listener.[141] And music has an ability to "attach" to memories, making it inseparable from our memories of important times in our lives. As we begin to come of age in our teenage years, our self-discovery is so emotionally charged that we remember deeply all that occurs then, which is why the music of our adolescence can instantly cause a flood of vivid memories.[142]

Interestingly, this element of beauty also has an unexpected link to order in the mathematical basis for an octave: When a note's frequency is doubled or halved, the resulting note sounds similar (creating an octave). The octave is so basic that even some animal species—monkeys and cats, for example—recognize it.[143] The ancient Greeks viewed the perfect fourth and perfect fifth, also mathematical ratios, as the basis of all music.[144] Reflecting this universal appeal, fourths and fifths are found in the music of a wide variety of cultural musical styles.[145]

Although music was evolutionarily advantaged and we derive pleasure from it, we are still left with a number of "whys." Why didn't evolution stop with the bare necessities of hearing and rhythmic storytelling? Why can some music call up such deep emotions in us? And why do so many feel a profound spiritual connection to music? Science can answer the how, but falls short in explaining the why of music. Evolutionary theory doesn't explain why we should have needed to develop such a strong emotional response to music. And neither science nor evolution is able to address music's strong link to spirituality.

Where does that leave us? With a universal and fundamental human desire which can't be rationally explained. With an experience that is often deeply emotional and meaningful, but not necessary to sustain life. With *something* that seems to be more important than it should.

# A Reflection on Beauty

*We live only to discover beauty. All else is a form of
waiting.*

—Kahlil Gibran

I once spent an emotional two weeks in a remote city
in northwest China. I was traveling to pick up our adopted daughter in the uneasy days following 9/11, in
a Muslim province bordering Afghanistan with a history of ethnic clashes with the government. To a girl
from the American Midwest, the place was *foreign*.
Remote even to the Chinese, the city I was visiting
was not geared to accommodate Western visitors. The
hotel and food were challenging, and no one save our
translator spoke English. The sun could not penetrate
the heavy industrial pollution; after an hour spent
outdoors, our throats hurt and eyes burned.

The way we spent our time did not improve upon the depressing environment; we had long waits in smoke-filled government offices for paperwork to be stamped; a bleak visit with the children left behind in the orphanage; and my new daughter sobbing herself to sleep after leaving the only mother she had known. We were hungry, stressed, and gloomy. As the bureaucratic process methodically came to a close, we were scheduled for a day trip to the nearby Tianshen Mountains. The contrast was stark. Majestic, wild, and unspoiled, the scenery we witnessed during the two-hour drive was spectacular. Colorful yurts, tent homes of the tribal Kazakh residents, were as scattered as their herds of wandering sheep.

At our destination waited a great treasure: glassy Heavenly Lake, nestled between snowy mountain peaks. It was the most beautiful sight I have ever seen. My memories of it still give me goose-bumps. The unforgettable image of a colorfully clad native on a horse and taking a ride in an enclosed boat on that amazing water completed our day. We were refreshed. I was aware, for the first time in my life, of how critical beauty is to my state of mind.

Where do we seek meaning from beauty? For some, it is snowshoeing or hiking in a beautiful part of nature. Others find it in art, architecture, or music. Beauty is even found in mathematics, as explained by John Polkinghorne, the former Cambridge physicist and Anglican priest:

> And we've found in theoretical physics that the fundamental laws of nature are always mathematically beautiful. In fact, if you've got some ugly equations, almost certainly you haven't got it right and you should think again. So beauty is the key to unlocking the secrets of the physical world.[146]

Some don't consciously seek it, never realizing why a favorite song or a sudden stumbled-upon treasure of nature puts a spring in their step. Many citizens of the world never get this experience. For the first time in human history, modern life has largely removed us from our intimate connection to nature's beauty. Many of us live in concrete buildings and work under fluorescent lighting with loud, ugly machinery. Those of us with means are able to decorate our artificial environment, partially offsetting our loss.

The poor in both developed and undeveloped countries alike often neither retain their historical connection to nature nor possess the means to make their environment aesthetically pleasing. Their everyday surroundings are dismal and depressing, with a lack of beauty permeating their lives, silently eating away their hope. We crave beauty to make our difficult lives more bearable, but why? There is no evolutionary advantage for enjoying beauty. It does not aid our physical survival; we are alone among the animals in this ability. There is no reason for it, and yet it exists. The real question is this: What is it we really crave? If there is no rational argument for this particularly human need, then isn't it possible that it is only a proxy for something else? We feel what Goethe called *selige sehnsucht*, or blessed longing, as the absence of that for which we long.[147] Plato believed that the true function of beauty is to lead us to something beyond—to help us glimpse reality itself—becoming "the true friend of God and as divine as any mortal may be."[148] The reality of which Plato spoke could well be the true nature of God.

# Part Three

# Love

# Chapter 6
# The Science of Love

*There is something in staying close to men and women and looking on them, and in the contact and odor of them that pleases the soul well. All things please the soul, but these please the soul well.*

—Walt Whitman

In Disney's animated movie *The Sword in the Stone*, Merlin described love as "the most powerful force in the universe."[149] Love has inspired art, music, and poetry. It has changed the course of history, and caused profound joy and unspeakable pain. Love is universal; anthropologists have found evidence of romantic love in almost 90 percent of 166 cultures surveyed.[150] Love clearly plays a central role in human existence, but why? Why does it exist, when lust alone, as in the rest of the animal world, is sufficient for reproduction? Scientists now believe we may be neurologically wired for love.

The word love comes from the Sanskrit word *lubh*, which means "to desire."[151] There are different types of love, each with a different evolutionary purpose and, as we are learning, with different neurological mechanisms. We experience three primary types of loving relationships: those that involve attachment, those that involve caregiving, and those that involve sex. Attachment is the longer-term fondness and security we develop, which fosters child rearing; caregiving is the instinctive impulse to protect and nurture children; and, obviously, sex is primarily for reproduction.[152]

As science dissects the basis for the feelings underlying the reproductive impulse, it is revealing a complex set of biochemical differences between lust—the desire for sexual gratification with any partner—and romantic love. Romantic love enables us to focus on one partner at a time, conserving time and energy.[153] Over time, romantic love settles into feelings of security, comfort, and calmness with our partner, which is attachment.[154] It is easy to see the evolutionary benefits of humans developing these emotions; let's explore their biological basis.

Primates first evolved social skills necessary for

living in groups for the advantages of allowing other members of the group to help provide the necessities of life.[155] The social brain systems grew in direct proportion to the bonds between humans; it may be the one characteristic that allowed homo sapiens to beat out other humanoid species.[156] One third of our genes govern brain function. Although we have only a few more genes than apes do, there is a significant difference in the way our brains function—a few hundred extra would create exponentially more connections.[157] Many of the parts of the human brain now shown to be related to love, including the caudate nucleus, the amygdala, and the hippocampus, are twice as big as those of the apes.[158]

And scientists have recently "rediscovered" a long known but previously not understood specialized brain cell, the von Economo neuron. This neuron is present in only a few species, including all great apes (including humans, but not the lesser apes), elephants, several species of whale, and the bottlenose dolphin. All of these species are social. The von Economo neurons are unusually large, often a sign of a high capacity for speed in the nervous system. One theory hypothesizes that they allow rapid assessment of volatile social situations, something that would be an evolutionary advantage within social species.

The specialized von Economo neurons exist only in the anterior cingulated cortex (ACC) and frontal insula (FI) portions of the brain. These portions of the brain appear to have roles in the emotions, particularly social emotions such as empathy, trust, and love. The FI, for example, becomes active when a mother hears a baby crying, or when someone studies a face to gauge intent. The ACC and FI also seem important to our ability to self-monitor our emotions, while the FI helps us with awareness of others. This link between self-awareness and the awareness of others makes it possible to understand others, enabling trusting relationships.[159] Our brains seem uniquely designed among species to enable highly complex social relationships.

We now know that love also includes powerful biological reinforcers. Our interactions with others—particularly those we spend the most time with and care the most about—impact us biologically, triggering the release of hormones that regulate multiple systems. Positive interactions impact our bodies positively, negative ones negatively.[160] And emotions "transmit" from one person to another. Studies have shown that simply observing others in an act causes the same neurons to fire in our own brains that would fire if we were performing the act ourselves. These "mirror neurons" cause emotions to be contagious, spreading from one to another.[161] Similarly, mimicking another, when spontaneous and not deliberate, can create positive feelings or rapport between two people.[162] Rapport, a positive interaction that strengthens bonds, requires mutual attention, shared positive feeling, and being in synch.[163]

Negative emotions are also contagious; babies who hear another baby cry in distress also start crying.[164] Distress signals in others trigger a biologic desire in us to help that person. We can ignore someone in need, but that requires us to suppress our own biologic impulse to help them.[165] So our brains are designed not just to allow interactions with others; it appears we are actually wired to care about them, too.

It also turns out that romantic love is literally addictive, triggering the activation of the same powerful opioid system that responds to heroin and is involved in other substance addictions.[166] Dopamine—the neurotransmitter associated with the brain's pleasure center and one of nature's most powerful stimulants—reinforces the positive emotions associated with having passionate love returned.[167] Dopamine also activates the same pathway as addictive drugs do, which is why many of the symptoms of love and drug abuse are the same, including obsession, cravings that are difficult to control, and the feeling of not being able to live without the object of desire.[168]

Romantic love also triggers lust, since dopamine triggers the release of testosterone.[169] Other hormones appear to drive other aspects of human love, including vasopressin, which governs the paternal instinct in male mammals, and oxytocin, which stimulates infant bonding as well as male-female attachment feelings.[170] Oxytocin, found in both men and women, decreases dopamine, which in turn decreases romantic feelings. This explains why, in the long run, love becomes attachment and leads to reduced passion as it matures.[171]

With love comes the desire for sexual exclusivity, which likely evolved to protect our genetic heritage, given the time and energy we spend attracting a mate. Yet, the desire for sex and sexual exclusivity are less important to those in love than the longing for emotional closeness.[172] While romantic love generally leads to lust, the reverse is not always true. Sexual gratification is often an end in itself in human behavior, although it can be a path toward love, as it triggers the same neurotransmitters that govern romantic love.[173]

It turns out there is also a biological basis behind attractiveness and our response to beauty, which has its own role to play in love. Beauty has proven to be fairly universal across cultures, and the most common characteristic of beauty is symmetry of features. Symmetry is considered beautiful by insects, animals, and people. Symmetry advertises a genetic superiority that has resisted imperfections, and we respond strongly to it. Looking at beautiful faces causes significant activity in the ventral tegmental area in the brain—an area rich in dopamine.[174] We can't help being attracted to beautiful people, and once attracted to them, we often can't help but fall in love.

So we appear to be wired to fall in love, and there are powerful biological reinforcers to dedicate ourselves to those with whom we fall in love. What can these relationships tell us about God? Deep relationships are forgiving and selfless; partners care more about the feelings of the other than they do about themselves. A good marriage can be one of the most rewarding human experiences and may be our best model for perfect love, the love we might expect to find in heaven. In heaven, free of our jealousy and possessiveness, we should be capable of having these meaningful relationships with everyone. These relationships may be only a pale preview of the kind of relationship we can expect with all other beings once in God's perfect home. C. S. Lewis believed that "the human loves can be glorious images of Divine love."[175]

# Chapter 7
# God Is Good for Us

*We're the only species that knows we're going to die.*
                                        —William Lobdell

It is easy to see the evolutionary advantages of the love we feel for our partners and for our children, but the evidence for natural selection working on whole populations—including the concept of altruism—is unsettled. While the research of some philosophers such as Elliot Sober supports an evolution of altruism, it is also true that putting our own needs or safety behind those of others could prove genetically disadvantageous. So why do we have concern for others?

Self-sacrifice is often associated with religious faith, with some level of belief in a next world, one that may include judgment. A belief in a next world can provide some incentive to give up comforts in this one for what one believes is right.[176] Inequality in society's rules and its impact on the powerless often leads to calls for social justice, which requires equal opportunity.[177] Faith communities from across the religious spectrum have long played visible, instrumental roles in social justice efforts. Christianity was one early example, promoting cultural, ethnic, and racial tolerance. Jesus's accepting the drink from the Samaritan woman, the parable of the good Samaritan, and Peter's baptism of the gentile Cornelius all demonstrated an (at-that-time) new message of tolerance.[178] Social justice is also an important element in Judaism and Islam. The "Holiness Code" in the Torah (Leviticus 19) outlines a commitment to fairness, human responsibility, and social justice.[179] Social justice is also fundamental to the teachings of the Qur'an, instructing that all human beings are the creatures of God, and wealth should be shared.[180]

Obviously we don't all begin our lives with equal opportunity. Even in capitalistic democracies that pride themselves on providing all citizens with opportunities to get ahead, studies show our rank in the socioeconomic hierarchy is more likely to be inherited than based on merit or achievement.[181] And studies have shown that the impact of socioeconomic inequality reaches beyond the financial. Anxiety and stress, felt disproportionately by those lower on the social scale, have strong negative correlations on health. Prolonged exposure to stress hormones, for example, depresses immune systems and stresses major systems like the cardiovascular.[182] Conversely, control over working conditions enjoyed by those at the higher end of the socioeconomic scale correlates to improved health and longer life.[183]

George Orwell saw society's growing unbelief in God as the most important factor at work in the modern world. Though an atheist himself, Orwell's concern was that society would lose its moral compass, with its inhabitants no longer afraid of justice after this life.[184] Orwell's concern was arguably justified: His lifetime included communism and Nazism, experiments in large-scale atheism that demonstrated what atrocities can occur when society loses its morality en masse. Perhaps it is these failures to find a purpose without God[185] that has helped lead to a recent resurgence of growth in virtually all the world's major religions, particularly in the developing world.[186] Faith helps drive us to care for and be just toward one another, and therefore to be healthier as a society.

There is evidence that faith drives not just healthier

societies but also healthier individuals. Studies now repeatedly show that self-indulgence in earthly pleasures may not bring happiness anyway.[187] In fact, they show that deep religious faith is healthy for us physically, leading to lower rates of heart disease, high blood pressure, and emphysema.[188] People with strong religious beliefs cope with stress better, have fewer addictions, are generally healthier, and may even live longer.[189]

There are also significant emotional benefits, with believers far less likely to commit suicide, abuse drugs or alcohol, be depressed, or divorce.[190] They are more likely to express satisfaction with their marriages and overall lives, and even recover from surgery more quickly.[191] Practices such as prayer and meditation significantly improve cognition and memory, and reduce anxiety, depression, and stress.[192]

Meditation—a concentrated focus on a mental object such as an idea or imagined sound or image, even if not religious—stimulates the anterior cingulated (AC) area of the brain. The AC has a major role in increasing social awareness and reducing anxiety and irritability.[193] By itself, most prayer has not been shown to have health benefits because it usually does not last long enough. When prayer is incorporated into longer, more intense meditation or into regular religious activity, health benefits, including increased cognition and even longer life, often result.[194]

Spiritual practices like meditation leave us feeling more relaxed, less stressed, and with a greater sense of security.[195] One study showed a 65-percent increase in dopamine, the same chemical released with cocaine use, in those who practiced yoga nidra, a state of yogic "sleep" in which the participant remains conscious and awake, but completely relaxed.[196] Another form of meditation, namely transcendental meditation, lowers the stress chemicals epinephrine and noepinephrine. Most major religions of the world, including Buddhism, Hinduism, and the religions of Abraham have a long history of meditation.

Additionally, spending significant time contemplating any grand theme actually changes our brains over time. Our brains constantly rearrange our neural circuitry in response to a wide variety of stimuli and events. Meditation—whether about God or something else—changes our brains in a unique way.[197] Researchers have found that people who have meditated more than ten years show asymmetrical activity in their thalamus: One side is more active than the other. This is almost never found in nonmeditators, except under certain medical conditions. The thalamus, a walnut-shaped part of our brain, is critical to our ability to determine what is and is not real. Researchers hypothesize that this change to the thalamus could indicate that what the long-term meditators concentrated on became more real to them. Since the thalamus doesn't distinguish between inner and outer reality, the more we think about God, *the more real he may become to us*.[198] This potentially outstanding finding could align science with the biblical adage to "seek and ye shall find."[199]

If faith is better for society and in our best interests as individuals, why doesn't everyone believe in God? The famous philosopher and mathematician Blaise Pascal described humans as being born with a God-shaped hole. We try to fill that hole with all sorts of things, but God alone will fill it.[200] Sometimes when we focus exclusively on our own desires, we can create pain in our lives. C.S. Lewis said pain can be God's tool: "Pain insists upon being attended to. God whispers to us in our pleasures, speaks in our conscience, but shouts in our pains: it is his megaphone to rouse a deaf world."[201]

Lewis, an avowed atheist early in his life, had a long and instructive journey to belief that he summarized this way:

If I find in myself a desire which no experience in this world can satisfy, the most probable explanation is that I was made for another world ... Earthly pleasures were never meant to satisfy it, but only to arouse it, to suggest the real thing. I must take care ... never to mistake them for the something else of which they are only a kind of copy, or echo, or mirage.[202]

Lewis found his proof for belief in the many "signposts" scattered throughout the universe that he believed pointed to God, and that included the "starry heavens above and the moral law within,"[203] a phrase coined by Kant and that represents a glimmer of God in each human being.[204] Lewis believed that abuse of free will led to the abuses of human history, "the long, terrible story of many trying to find something other than God which will make him happy. God created things which had free will—and free will, though it makes evil possible, is also the only thing that makes possible any love or joy worth having."[205]

Science now increasingly seems to indicate that following God can be good for us. Why are we, alone among the animals, better off pursuing *something* beyond the daily grind of survival and reproduction? We have always been driven to fill a void we cannot fully explain. While God himself may be unknowable, his commandments and how to follow him are not. There is little variance among the world's great religions on a moral law. When we follow it, generally good things happen in our lives. When we do not, we may suffer the consequences.[206]

# Chapter 8
# The Face of God

*It is far more comforting to think God listened and said no, than to think that nobody's out there.*

—Albert Lewis

Genesis states God created us "in his own image."[207] The reference to "his image" likely refers to our possession of free will as the characteristic that most distinguishes us from God's other creations. Only humans know right from wrong and are able to make choices about the type of life to live. Without free will, we would be as slaves to God, serving without choice. Could we still love God without the choice to serve him? A master-slave relationship does not foster genuine love. Affection is possible, but the lack of choice inevitably causes at least some resentment, hindering the formation of a deep, true love.

Why would God grant us the unique privilege of being in a loving relationship with him? Think about our own children. We love them possibly more than we love ourselves. We want the best for them. We do everything in our power to equip them to make good choices, knowing that the time will come when they will be independent. But it is not easy. They fail as they test their wings, they hurt when they fail, and we hurt with them. When they succeed, their successes are more gratifying than our own. While it is tempting to want to make their decisions to help them avoid pain, we know they must make their own choices because we love them.

By describing God as our heavenly Father, the Bible gives us a direct parallel of God's feelings toward us. Free will requires consequences for wrong choices or it wouldn't really be free will. Once again thinking of a human parent, don't we search for ways to help our children make things right when they do wrong? Even when they can't undo their actions, often all we hope for is their sincere acknowledgement that they've realized their mistakes. A God without love would be vengeful and punitive. A God who loves would provide a means of redemption.

There has, however, always been a significant obstacle to the "God is love" theory: If God truly loves us, why does he allow suffering? This is one of the deepest of philosophical questions, and according to many thinkers, the answer also points to free will. If free will gives us choices but God always intervenes to prevent any negative consequences from those choices, then the choices were not real choices. We could eat too much, drink too much, abuse our relationships, and nothing bad would happen. Our choices would not matter: We could do anything we want today, and tomorrow start over again, as if yesterday's choice never happened.

But what about suffering that does not result from choices we make, such as suffering from disease or natural disasters? Again, according to some thinkers, the answer seems to come back to free will, and not just to choice in our actions but also in our beliefs. As the physicist John Polkinghorne puts it, "God is not the puppet master of the universe, pulling every string. God has taken, if you like, a risk."[208] If God visibly and routinely interceded to prevent terrible things outside our control from happening, we would have no choice but to believe in him. We would become accustomed to seeing evidence of him and might not seek him out—we may even take him for granted.

We may not wrestle with the choice to love him as he loves us, freely and completely. Love requires choice, and God profoundly wants us to choose loving him. Love is limiting; we must give up some freedom to be in a relationship, but it is worth it. This is true of having a relationship with God.[209]

Love has three primary characteristics. First, real love is obsessive and without reason, as we love our mates or our children. God's love seems obsessive and without reason. Why would an omnipotent being capable of creating the grandiosity of the entire universe create tiny, fragile, and morally weak creatures and then invest so much care in them? Why would he ensure that we somehow receive his message that he loves us? Most of all, why would he love us?

Second, real love is sacrificial. We care more about the feelings and needs of those we love deeply than we do about our own feelings and needs. Human history is filled with examples of extreme sacrifice, from a soldier's sacrifice for a comrade in a foxhole, to complete strangers sacrificing themselves for others. God's redemption—our own undeserved forgiveness for our multitude of sins and weaknesses—sacrificially overlooks our obligation that we pay the price for our sins.

Finally, while very strong, real love has a breaking

point. Relationships can be breached beyond repair; wrongs can be extreme enough to cause permanent damage that cannot be healed. The Bible says that our sin is enough to separate us from God eternally.[210] Just as we heal a strained human relationship first by repenting (we can't be forgiven if we continue our offense), and second by reaching out in forgiveness for forgiveness, we can gain God's redemption. These human steps mirror the teachings of major religions toward repentance.

Love also provides us a shot at immortality, and not just through heaven. Rabbi Albert Lewis described being forgotten after we have died as the "second death," referencing this poem by Thomas Hardy:

They count as quite forgot,
They are as men who have existed not,
Theirs is a loss past loss of fitful breath
It is the second death.[211]

Relationships with and sacrifice for others, through love, is our best legacy. One example can be found in the closest surrogate for heavenly love we can find here on Earth: family. We dedicate our lives to another person to whom we are devoted beyond explanation. We create offspring whom we love often more than anything else in this life. We sacrifice much to care for, protect, teach and nurture our children in hopes they will thrive and, in turn, repeat the cycle. We leave this world knowing we left something permanent and significant behind. Our lives were not meaningless, and we will not be forgotten.

Earthly loves provide us with a model of how to love God. Free will allows us the gift of choosing to love God. In exchange, perfect love—unhindered by human jealousies, hurts or fears—may wait for us when we go to our final home with God. Being surrounded by infinite and immeasurable love seems likely to be the most important quality we will experience in heaven. The small glimpses we see here on Earth give us only the most sparing insights into what we can expect in God's heaven: nothing less than overwhelming love and peace.

# A Reflection on Love

*I have found the paradox, that if you love until it hurts,
there can be no more hurt, only more love.*

—Mother Teresa

Years ago I worked with an accounting manager
named Lon. He joined the company where I worked,
and—I'm now ashamed to admit—I found him a
little irritating. Older than I, nerdy, with glasses and
thinning hair, he always had a smile on his face and a
spring in his step. I didn't work with him closely, and
he didn't stay long. After a couple of years he quit his
job to become a missionary. I was shocked. I was thirty, aggressive, and career-minded, dedicated to con-
tinuing my upward climb. Nobody I had ever known
had quit a decent corporate job, taking such a significant risk with a start-up missionary group. It didn't
make any sense to me.

Lon wasn't an important part of my life, and I quickly forgot him. A decade later, a friend who had stayed in touch with him forwarded me an email: Lon had been diagnosed with a serious illness and was sharing his journey via newsletter. For reasons I can't explain, I sent him a note expressing sympathy and asking to be added to his newsletter subscription. For the next eighteen months, I was a bystander to his experiences: the hope of new treatments, the medical setbacks, but mostly his deep faith and optimism.

That impulse proved to have a profound impact on my life. Today I can't remember a single email, though I wish I had saved them all. It doesn't matter: Lon was the first example in my life of someone who *really* had the religious faith I'd always heard about but hadn't grow up with and didn't understand. His faith never wavered, even when his condition deteriorated enough so that he considered a high-risk treatment with long odds. His faith was contagious; I remember thinking surely someone with that much faith must have their prayers answered.

Lon's positive, regular emails always brightened my day. One day when I was sitting at my desk at work, I opened one of those emails, written not by Lon but by his wife, Jane. Lon's battle was suddenly over. I closed my office door and cried, for a man I had barely known and had not seen in ten years. It was difficult for me to make sense of his death. What good was Lon's faith when it didn't save him? What about all the prayers said on his behalf by so many people? Why had all those prayers seemed to offer the experimental treatment that gave Lon and his family so much hope? I had no answers.

I now realize faith doesn't guarantee that nothing bad will happen to us. As individuals, it does alter the quality of our lives and, in Lon's case, it can also alter the quality of others' lives. Many of us have been fortunate enough to have had the gift of people who leave disproportionate-sized holes in our lives when they are gone. Lon was one such person for me.

I have been blessed with at least two others. My earliest memories as a child include my maternal grandparents. We lived close to them, and my sister and I were at their home often; it was our second home. My grandmother was an outstanding cook of the fried chicken, mashed potatoes, and home-made pie variety. My grandfather, Howard Jennings Kaufman, was a large, quiet man, a German Mennonite. For a man of few words, he played an oversized role in my childhood. I don't recall him playing games with us or passing on any life lessons, at least not with words. Instead, as I look back, I see that he simply *loved us unconditionally*. To this day, I can't really explain why I say that. It had to be in the way he lit up when we came into the room, the way he interacted with us. It was just there.

I watched in the last decade of his life as diabetes cost him first one leg and then the other, cutting the once-independent man literally in half. Only at the very end did he lose the light that sparked when I walked into the room; I knew then that his time was up. I was almost thirty when he died; over the next ten years, I cried every time I thought of him.

I was also lucky in my father-in-law. Gordon Eugene McCleary was the only child of an alcoholic Irishman and his tiny spitfire wife. One day, she told him he had a choice: It was the booze or her. He chose her, but passed the alcoholism on to my father-in-law. Gordon was a B-24 gunner in World War II. Family legend has it that he promised God that if his life was spared in the war, he would have a large family. He kept his word. He and Pauline had fourteen children: twelve sons and two daughters. The large family was always poor, even more so after a bad back put him on disability by the age of fifty, with the last five kids, including my husband, Russ, still at home.

Russ says he feels blessed; he had a home and family, and he always knew he was loved. Beyond that, however, his childhood was far from ideal. Occasionally hungry, never owning new clothes, and with his father sometimes violent when drunk, he learned survival tactics as a child that impact him today. By the time I met him, Gordon had mellowed. He never gave up drinking, but the violence had stopped. For some reason, he liked me— I mean, really liked me. To this day, I have no idea why. For the second time in my life, there it was again: *unconditional love*. He treated all of his kids that way. When the recurrence of lung cancer finally took him, he left a giant hole in our lives.

We all have big regrets in our lives; in the twenty-five years I knew Gordon, I never once told him I loved him, even when I visited him in the hospital knowing the end was near. Now I have to live with the belief—more of a faith really—that although I never said it, he somehow knew, knew from the fact that I visited him regularly all of the twenty-five years I knew him; knew from the fact that I carefully chose his birthday and Christmas presents from a deep understanding of who he was and what he would enjoy; knew from the fact that as my husband and I grew more financially secure, we ensured he and Pauline were comfortable in their well-deserved retirement. Gordon and I didn't have to say it to know it—we both just knew.

Who have you had in your life who loved you unconditionally? What difference has that relationship made, and how diminished would your life have been without it? We seem designed to love, more than simply for reproduction's sake. Our love for each other, forgiving and selfless, is a model for paradise. God seems to be good for us, as individuals and as societies. The Bible says that God himself is love[212] evidenced by our very consciousness, by the choice he has given us to seek him. Love truly is the most powerful force in the universe. We can assume that heaven must contain more love than we are able to imagine. We can rest assured knowing that God's overwhelming, unconditional love will be there when we join him in his home.

# Conclusion

# Chapter 9
# What It All Means

*Hope is necessary in every condition. The miseries of poverty, sickness, of captivity, would, without this comfort, be insupportable. Life is hard. A belief that there is a heaven, a good something after death, tells us that not only will we not cease to exist when we die but, more importantly, that our efforts in this life are not in vain.*
—Samuel Johnson

Our exploration has hinted at the nature of heaven based on what can be found here on Earth. We started first by addressing a belief in God; without God, heaven doesn't make much sense. None of the results of science, the reflections of philosophy, examples of beauty in the world can ever prove the existence of God; they can only cause us to wonder, to question, and—if we are open to it—to believe that we see signs of God in our world, signs put there for us to find if we are open to seeing them. It is, however, a circular search: We see evidence of God only if we are open to seeing it. Before we can see this evidence, we must first have faith enough to be open to it. The choice is ours, a gift of free will allowing us to choose. We must choose to seek God. It's that simple and that difficult all at once. On our search, we can never *know*—we are required to take a leap of faith. That seems to be God's only requirement from us: taking a first step, choosing to look for him. Love always requires first making the choice to love.

Once we believe in God, his heaven is likely orderly and rational, not random and unpredictable. The universe seems unbelievably fine-tuned for our existence. It appears to have been designed to make us possible. We were made to be curious, with the whole of creation a playground perfectly made for us to explore. The universe is infinitely vast and complex, more than enough to spend an eternity discovering. It is orderly, enabling us to find the grand design behind it. Heaven must also be beautiful, far more than we can imagine. The very best of this world—nature, art, music—must be even more wonderful in God's home. We crave beauty, a proxy for God. Somehow beauty turns us to God, allowing us to glimpse him, however dimly. Lastly, heaven must be full of love, considerably beyond what we can experience in this life. Death is our final gift. Only with it are we redeemed—if we seek to be. Only after death can we return to God, to find, as Rabbi Al Lewis said, "a happiness you cannot find alone."[213]

Thus God has his plan to draw us toward him, using the order, beauty, and love around us to point to himself. If we find him, we fulfill our lives and our purpose. We have our part to play in his plan. The fundamental purpose of each of our lives is to determine whether we will seek God. We are destined to search. We have free will, with the freedom to choose. If we are open to it, we will see. If we see, we will believe. If we believe, we will be fulfilled. We are required to take the initial leap of faith, of being willing to believe. If we do, we can see the breadcrumb trail God has left us, the reflection of heaven all around us. We live in Plato's best possible world. We can find it. We are driven to seek it.

*Heav'n's morning breaks, and earth's vain shadows flee ...*
—Henry Lyte, "Abide with Me"

# Epilogue

Proceeds of this book will go to groups supporting orphans, such as the Hope Healing Home in Beijing, which cares for sick and physically disabled babies who have been abandoned. Dr. Joyce Hill and her husband, Robin, provide care and medical treatment for babies with surgically correctable deformities. These babies are looked after in their own home and are treated as if they were their own children. The Hills have also established several centers in China that care for babies that have severe deformities and are born with conditions that are incompatible with prolonged life. Their mission in these centers is this: to comfort always, to relieve often, and to save sometimes. You can learn more about their work in the book *The House of Hope: God's Love for the Abandoned Orphans of China*, by Elisabeth Gifford, or at the New Hope Foundation's website:

http://www.hopefosterhome.com/index.html

# Acknowledgements

I wish I could thank each of the hundreds of people who have played meaningful roles in my life, since you have all shaped this book. But I would fail, and so must stick to thanking the handful of those who have had the most impact.

Barry Mongan, while undergoing his own significant life journey, generously offered his precious time to provide important editing. You gave just what was needed: a keen auditor's eye, and a kind skeptic's heart. Your many contributions simply made this book much better than it was. I know Anna also provided editing support—I am incredibly grateful to you both. (A "shout out" to Patrick and Richard!)

I was convinced that a chance introduction in Tokyo meant that Ann Ness was to be this book's editor. Luckily for me, she turned out instead to be my agent and chief cheerleader. Thank you, Ann, for your unbelievably generous response to someone who was a stranger a few months earlier. You are a good witness for your faith.

Thank you, Maria Kochiras and Annie Jones, not only for providing me feedback on the first draft, but even more valuably for being my good friends. You have always provided me a safe place to share and laugh, even when through tears. Thank you both for being you.

Thanks to Cindy Tade for being my best friend the last twenty years. Where did the time go?

My parents, Bob and Kathy Welch, are the reason this book was possible. They gave me everything I needed and are the source of whatever talents I possess. I am blessed to have you as my parents. To my second parents, Gordon and Pauline McCleary I thank you for loving me as a daughter. I miss you both every day.

Thank you, Bryan, for your willingness to read the early draft and correct your mother's mistakes. Thanks to Megan and Claire for teaching me the true meaning of family. I have always felt blessed not just to love all three of you as my children but also to genuinely like you as really cool people. And my deepest gratitude to Russ, the love of my life, for not telling me I was crazy when I told you I was going to write this book. Your unwavering support throughout this three-year journey has made all the difference in the world.

Most importantly, a humble thank you to this book's true Author. All flaws are mine alone. I am staggeringly grateful for the considerable blessing of the task You saw fit to assign to me. May Your purpose for it be fulfilled.

# Discussion Questions

1. *The Best Possible World* makes three assumptions:
   a. God exists.
   b. God is consistent and transparent.
   c. God wants to be found.

   Do these assumptions seem reasonable to you? Why or why not?

2. The world's major religions have widely varying views about heaven, from Islam's very physical place of comforts to Judaism's intellectual realm to Buddhism's enlightenment. Where do you believe religions got their views of heaven from, and why are these views so different?

3. The view that the good on Earth may be a reflection of heaven is old and has been advocated by a variety of people with differing philosophies

and backgrounds. Does this idea ring true to you?
Why or why not?

4. In their book *A Meaningful World*, Wiker and
Witt maintain that the world must have an underlying order in for scientific activity to be fruit-
ful. Discuss your own observations about the
order (or lack of order) you see in the world.

5. Some prominent scientists believe that the fifteen
or so physical constants that make our universe
possible appear to be finely tuned, indicating the
possibility of a divine creator. Yet others, including the notable Stephen Hawking, have publicly
stated they do not believe God was necessary for
the emergence of the universe. Discuss why you
believe leaders in these advanced academic areas
can disagree about what the scientific evidence is
telling them.

6. Humans and mice share much of the same DNA,
including the mutations called *ancient repetitive
elements* (AREs), leading some scientists to point
in the direction of a common ancestor. Discuss

your own beliefs about evolution and how you came to those beliefs.

7. Art and beauty add meaning to many people's lives. Discuss how they do so in yours.

8. Music's ability to "attach" to memories can make it meaningful in our lives. Discuss the period of your life from which your favorite music derives and why you think this music has such an appeal for you.

9. Love may be one of the easiest "echoes" of heaven to understand, given our general understanding that God is love. Discuss why you believe that love in this life is so often flawed and causes pain.

10. With studies showing that a belief in God is beneficial to the health and well-being of individuals, discuss why you believe more people don't live strong lives of faith.

11. God's granting free will to us and the seemingly random nature of human events could explain the

bad things that happen in this world, one of the most significant obstacles for many nonbelievers. How well do you feel that the theory of free will addresses the evil and suffering in the world? Discuss the reasons for your views.

12. Discuss what an impact unconditional love can have on our lives or the lives of those we love.

13. *The Best Possible World* lays out evidence to support the claim that, since we derive meaning from three areas—order, beauty, and love—these areas may reveal aspects of God himself and his home. Are there other things in life beyond these three areas from which you draw meaning?

# Bibliography

Albom, Mitch. *Have a Little Faith*. New York: Hyperion, 2009

Barnett, Lincoln. *The Universe and Dr. Einstein*. Mineola, NY: Dover Publications, 1948.

Barry, Brian. *Why Social Justice Matters*. Cambridge UK: Polity Press, 2005.

Belin, David W. "Jewish Concern for 'TZEDAKAH' (Charity) and Social Justice," in *Choosing Judaism: An Opportunity for Everyone*. http://joi.org/library/pubs/belin.shtml (2008).

Chen, Ingfei. "The Social Brain." *Smithsonian Magazine* (June 2009), 38-43.

Chopelas, Peter. "Heaven and Hell in the Afterlife, According to the Bible." http://aggreen.net/beliefs/heaven_hell.html.

Chestnut, Glenn F. "The God-Shaped Hole in the Human Soul." http://hindsfoot.org/godsha.html.

Collins, Francis S. *The Language of God*. New York: Free Press, 2006.

Dewey, John. *Art As Experience*. New York: Penguin Group, 1934.

Fisher, Helen. *Why We Love: The Nature and Chemistry of Romantic Love*. New York: Holt, 2004.

Gardner, Howard. *Art, Mind, and Brain: A Cognitive Approach to Creativity*. New York: Basic Books, 1982.

Gingerich, Owen. *God's Universe*. Cambridge, MA: Belknap Press, 2006.

Glynn, Patrick. *God The Evidence: The Reconciliation of Faith and Reason in a Postsecular World*. New York: Three Rivers Press, 1997.

Goleman, Daniel. *Social Intelligence*. New York: Bantam Dell, 2006.

Hawking, Stephen. *A Brief History of Time*. New York: Bantam Press, 1998.

Hugo, Victor. *The Hunchback of Notre Dame.* New York: Barnes and Noble Classics, 2004 (Paris, 1831).

Janson, H. W. *History of Art: A Survey of the Major Visual Arts from the Dawn of History to the Present Day*. New York: Harry N. Abrams, 1974.

———. *The Mirror of History*. New York: Time-Life Library of Arts, 1966.

Jastrow, Robert. *God and the Astronomers*. New York: W. W. Norton, 1992.

Johnson, Christopher Jay and Marsha G. McGee, eds. *How Different Religions View Death and the Afterlife*. Philadelphia: The Charles Press, 1998.

Keller, Timothy. *The Reason for God*. New York: Penguin Group, 2008.

Kimmelman, Michael. *The Accidental Masterpiece: On the Art of Life and Vice Versa*. New York: Penguin Books, 2005.

Kruschwitz, Robert B. *Christianity and Islam: Christian Reflection, a Series in Faith and Ethics*. Waco, TX: Baylor University, 1989.

Lebedoff, David. "Imagine There's No Heaven . . ." *Minneapolis Star Tribune*, April 5, 2009.

Levitin, Daniel J. *This Is Your Brain on Music: The Science of a Human Obsession*. New York: Penguin Group, 2006.

Lewis, C. S. *The Four Loves*. New York: Harcourt Brace and Company, 1960.

Lloyd, G. E. R. *Early Greek Science: Thales to Aristotle*. New York: W. W. Norton and Company, 1970.

Male, Emile. *The Gothic Image: Religious Art in France of the Thirteenth Century*. New York: Harper & Row, 1972.

Meyer, Leonard B. *Emotion and Meaning in Music.* Chicago: The University of Chicago Press, 1956.

Newberg, Andrew. "This is Your Brain on Religion." *USA Today,* June 15, 2009.

Newberg, Andrew and Mark Robert Waldman. *How God Changes Your Brain. Breakthrough Findings from a Leading Neuroscientist.* New York: Ballantine Books, 2009.

Nicholi, Armand M., Jr. *The Question of God: C. S. Lewis and Sigmund Freud Debate God, Love, Sex, and the Meaning of Life.* New York: Free Press, 2002.

Sacks, Oliver. *Musicophilia.* New York: Vintage Books, 2007.

Schroeder, Gerald L. *The Science of God: The Convergence of Scientific and Biblical Wisdom.* New York: Broadway Books, 1997.

Tippett, Krista. *Einstein's God: Conversations about Science and the Human Spirit.* New York: Penguin Books, 2010.

Trueblood, Elton. *The Common Ventures of Life.* New York: Harper, 1949.

Wiker, Benjamin and Jonathan Witt. *A Meaningful World: How the Arts and Sciences Reveal the Genius of Nature.* Downers Grove, IL: InterVarsity Press, 2006.

# Endnotes

1. Christopher Jay Johnson and Marsha G. McGee, eds., *How Different Religions View Death and the Afterlife* (Philadelphia: The Charles Press, 1998), 249–258.
2. Johnson and McGee, 142.
3. Johnson and McGee, 149.
4. Johnson and McGee, 199.
5. Peter Chopelas, *Heaven and Hell in the Afterlife, According to the Bible.*
6. Johnson and McGee, 50.
7. Johnson and McGee, 115, 122.
8. 1 Corinthians 2:9.
9. John 14:2.
10. Romans 14:17.
11. "Behold, the Heaven and the Heaven of Heavens is the Lord's thy God, the earth also, with all that therein is." Deuteronomy 10:14; "Thus saith the Lord, The Heaven is my throne, and the earth is my footstool." Isaiah 66:1.
12. "The Heavens declare the glory of God; and the firmament sheweth His handiwork." Psalms 19:1.
13. "Rejoice, and be exceeding glad: for great is your reward in Heaven." Matthew 5:12; "And the Lord shall deliver me from every evil work, and will preserve me unto His Heavenly kingdom." 2 Timothy 4:18.

14. "... the kingdom of Heaven is like unto treasure hid in a field." Matthew 13:44.

15. Matthew 13:46.

16. Romans 1 and Jesus' parables in Luke 7:41–43, 12:47–48, and 19:12–27, per Johnson and McGee, 43.

17. Revelations 2:7.

18. Matthew 25:46.

19. Matthew 5:19.

20. "Verily I say unto you, Except ye be converted and become as little children, ye shall not enter into the kingdom of Heaven." Matthew 18:3.

21. Matthew 13:37–43.

22. Matthew 3:12.

23. Matthew 13:49–50.

24. Matthew 10:28.

25. Johnson and McGee, 70.

26. Elton Trueblood, *The Common Ventures of Life* (New York: Harper, 1949), 104ff.

27. G. E. R. Lloyd, *Early Greek Science: Thales to Aristotle* (New York: W.W. Norton, 1970), 72.

28. Gerald L. Schroeder, *The Science of God: The Convergence of Scientific and Biblical Wisdom* (New York: Broadway Books, 1997), 73.

29. Lloyd, 8.

30. Lincoln Barnett, *The Universe and Dr. Einstein* (Mineola: Dover Publications, Inc., 1948), 15.

31. Francis S. Collins, *The Language of God* (New York: Free Press, 2006), 6.

32. Lloyd, 131–2.

33. Benjamin Wiker and Jonathan Witt, *A Meaningful World: How the Arts and Sciences Reveal the Genius of Nature* (Downers Grove IL: InterVarsity Press, 2006), 96.

34. Wiker and Witt, 145.

35. Timothy Keller, *The Reason for God* (New York: Penguin Group, 2008), x.

36. Friedrich Nietzsche, *The Gay Science*, Section 108.

37. Lloyd, 79, 97.

38. Lloyd, 67.

39. Wiker and Witt, 180.

40. Wiker and Witt, 50.

41. Robert Jastrow, *God and the Astronomers* (New York: W.W. Norton, 1992), 115.

42. Owen Gingerich, *God's Universe* (Cambridge, MA: Belknap Press, 2006), 49.

43. Wiker and Witt, 153.

44. Collins, 74. A complete list of the conditions necessary to create a universe capable of supporting life can be found in John Leslie's book *Universes*.

45. Patrick Glynn, *God The Evidence: The Reconciliation of Faith and Reason in a Postsecular World* (New York: Three Rivers Press, 1997), 22–23.

46. Stephen Hawking, *A Brief History of Time* (New York: Bantam Press, 1998), 127.

47. Gingerich, 58.

48. Gingerich, 12.

49. Jastrow, 106–107.

50. Collins, 66–67.

51. Schroeder, 23.

52. Glynn, 47.

53. Wiker and Witt, 181–183.
54. Collins, 90.
55. Collins, 94.
56. Glynn, 47–48.
57. Keller, 93.
58. Collins, 124.
59. Gingerich, 65.
60. Collins, 137–138.
61. Gingerich, 100.
62. Gingerich, 118.
63. Collins, 23.
64. Gingerich, 109.
65. C. S. Lewis, *The Four Loves* (New York: Harcourt Brace, 1960), 20–21.
66. Glynn, 19.
67. Tippett, 6.
68. Tippett, 20.
69. Collins, 63.
70. Keller, 127.
71. Keller, 140.
72. Collins, 176.
73. Gingerich, 12.
74. Krista Tippett, host of the public radio series *Speaking of Faith*, goes further to say that "the suggestion that science and religion are incompatible makes no sense at all." Tippett, 5.
75. Keller, 132.
76. Jastrow, 114.
77. Victor Hugo, *The Hunchback of Notre Dame* (New York: Barnes and Noble Classics, 2004), 374.

78. H. W. Janson, *The History of Art: A Survey of the Major Visual Arts from the Dawn of History to the Present Day* (New York: Harry N. Abrams, 1974), 10–16.

79. Emile Male, *The Gothic Image: Religious Art in France of the Thirteenth Century* (New York: Harper & Row, 1972), vii.

80. Hugo, 176.

81. Howard Gardner, *Art, Mind, and Brain: A Cognitive Approach to Creativity* (Basic Books, 1982), 36.

82. John Dewey, *Art As Experience* (New York: Penguin Group, 1934), 84.

83. Dewey, 339–40.

84. Dewey, 90.

85. Dewey, 341.

86. Dewey, 5.

87. Janson, *The Mirror of History*, 6.

88. Dewey, 339.

89. Dewey, 7–8.

90. Dewey, 8.

91. Gardner, 36–37.

92. Dewey, 354.

93. Dewey, 13.

94. Dewey, 165.

95. Dewey, 25–26.

96. Michael Kimmelman, *The Accidental Masterpiece: On the Art of Life and Vice Versa* (New York: Penguin Books, 2005), 62.

97. Gardner, 43.

98. Dewey, 44.

99. Dewey, 98–99.

100. Dewey, 91.

101. Gardner, 87–88.

102. Gardner, 212.

103. Gardner, 210.

104. Gardner, 86–87.

105. Kimmelman, 220–221.

106. Kimmelman, 220.

107. Matthew 18:3.

108. Janson, *The History of Art*, 17.

109. Dewey, 49.

110. Dewey, 112–113.

111. Dewey, 70–71.

112. Dewey, 123–127.

113. Daniel J. Levitin, *This Is Your Brain on Music: The Science of a Human Obsession* (New York: Penguin Group, 2006), 6.

114. Kimmelman, 6.

115. Levitin, 44.

116. Levitin, 254–260.

117. Oliver Sacks, *Musicophilia* (New York: Vintage Books, 2007), 259.

118. Sacks, 266.

119. Levitin, 261.

120. Sacks, 102.

121. Sacks, 34.

122. Sacks, xii.

123. Levitin, 29.

124. Sacks, 152.

125. Levitin, 184.

126. Sacks, 379.

127. Levitin, 191.

128. Sacks, 152.

129. Sacks, 385.

130. Meyer, 19.
131. Meyer, 27–28.
132. Meyer, 30–35.
133. Levitin, 125.
134. Levitin, 191.
135. Levitin, 236–237.
136. Levitin, 230.
137. Levitin, 38.
138. Levitin, 38.
139. Sacks, 106.
140. Levitin, 243–245.
141. Dewey, 113.
142. Levitin, 231–234.
143. Levitin, 31.
144. Levitin, 31–32.
145. Leonard B. Meyer, *Emotion and Meaning in Music* (Chicago: The University of Chicago Press, 1956), 63.
146. Tippett, 256-7.
147. Keller, 134.
148. Dewey, 303.
149. *The Sword in the Stone*, directed by Wolfgang Reitherman (Los Angeles: Walt Disney Studios, 1963).
150. Helen Fisher, *Why We Love: The Nature and Chemistry of Romantic Love* (New York: Henry Holt, 2004), 30.
151. Fisher, 20.
152. Goleman, 189.
153. Fisher, xiv.
154. Fisher, 87.
155. Goleman, 323.
156. Goleman, 329.
157. Fisher, 148.

158. Fisher, 149.

159. Ingfei Chen, "The Social Brain," *Smithsonian Magazine* (June 2009): 40–41.

160. Goleman, 5.

161. Goleman, 41–42.

162. Goleman, 31.

163. Goleman, 29.

164. Goleman, 55.

165. Goleman, 55.

166. Goleman, 192.

167. Fisher, 76.

168. Fisher, 182.

169. Fisher, 83.

170. Fisher, 89.

171. Fisher, 91–92.

172. Fisher, 21–22.

173. Fisher, 85.

174. Fisher, 105–106.

175. Lewis, 9.

176. Keller, 67.

177. Brian Barry, *Why Social Justice Matters* (Cambridge UK: Polity Press, 2005), 140, 200.

178. Glynn, 151–153.

179. David W. Belin, *Choosing Judaism: An Opportunity for Everyone*.

180. Robert B. Kruschwitz, *Christianity and Islam* (Waco, TX: Baylor University, 1989), 40.

181. Barry, 17.

182. Barry, 77.

183. Barry, 80.

184. David Lebedoff, "Imagine There's No Heaven . . .," *Minneapolis Star Tribune*, April 5, 2009.
185. Glynn, 166.
186. Keller, 6.
187. Glynn, 76–77.
188. Glynn, 80–81.
189. Andrew Newberg. "This is Your Brain on Religion," *USA Today*, June 15, 2009.
190. Glynn, 63–64.
191. Glynn, 63–64.
192. Newberg.
193. Andrew Newberg and Mark Robert Waldman, *How God Changes Your Brain. Breakthrough Findings from a Leading Neuroscientist* (New York: Ballantine Books, 2009), 124–125.
194. Newberg and Waldman, 28–29.
195. Newberg and Waldman, 55–56.
196. Newberg and Waldman, 55.
197. Glynn, 81.
198. Newberg and Waldman, 54–55.
199. Matthew 7:7.
200. Glenn F. Chestnut, *The God-Shaped Hole in the Human Soul.*
201. Nicholi, 213.
202. Nicholi, 47.
203. Nicholi, 37.
204. Collins, 29.
205. Nicholi, 40.
206. Glynn, 169.
207. Albom, 82.

208. Tippett, 269.
209. Keller, 49.
210. Isiah 59:2.
211. Mitch Albom, *Have a Little Faith* (New York: Hyperion, 2009), 127.
212. 1 John 4:8.
213. Albom, 145.